Watching Lions

in Africa

Louise and Richard Spilsbury

Heinemann Library
Chicago, Illinois

© 2006 Heinemann Library
a division of Reed Elsevier Inc.
Chicago, Illinois

Customer Service 888-454-2279
Visit our website at www.heinemannraintree.com

Designed by Ron Kamen and edesign
Illustrations by Martin Sanders
Printed and bound in China by South China Printing Company

10 09 08 07 06
10 9 8 7 6 5 4 3 2 1

Library of Congress Cataloging-in-Publication Data
Spilsbury, Louise.
  Watching lions in Africa / Louise and Richard Spilsbury.
    p. cm. -- (Wild world)
  Includes bibliographical references and index.
  ISBN 1-4034-7222-X (library binding - hardcover : alk. paper) -- ISBN 1-4034-7235-1 (pbk. : alk. paper)
  1. Lions--Africe--Juvenile literature. I. Spilsbury, Richard, 1963- II Title. III. Series: Wild world (Chicago, Ill.)
QL737.C23S585 2006
599.757'096--dc22
                                        2005016776

Acknowledgments
The author and publishers are grateful to the following for permission to reproduce copyright material: Alamy Images pp. 4 (Mike Hill), 7 (Chris Fredriksson), 18 (Mike Hill), 19 (Steve Bloom Pictures), 24 (Images of Africa Photobank); Ardea pp. 5 (Francois Gohier), 9 (Yann Arthus Bertrand), 11 (Chris Harvey), 16 (Ferrero-Labat), 23 (Chris Harvey), 25 (Chris Knights), 26 (Chris Harvey); Corbis pp. 10, 15 (DiMaggio, Kalish), 20 (Fritz Polking), 27 (W. Perry Conway), 28 (Philip Perry), 29 (Kevin Schafer); FLPA p. 21 (Colin Elsey); Getty Images p. 14; Nature PL p. 17 (Anup Shah); NHPA pp. 8 (Ann & Steve Toon), 22 (Jonathan & Angela Scott); PhotoLibrary.com p. 13 (Tim Jackson); Still Pictures p. 12 (Martin Harvey). Cover photograph of lioness with cubs reproduced with permission of FLPA/Fritz Polking.

The publishers would like to thank Michael Bright for his assistance in the preparation of this book. Every effort has been made to contact copyright holders of any material reproduced in this book. Any omissions will be rectified in subsequent printings if notice is given to the publishers. The paper used to print this book comes from sustainable resources.

Some words are shown in bold, **like this**. You can find out what they mean by looking in the glossary.

Contents

Meet the Lions

This is Africa, the home of lions. Lions are some of the biggest cats in the world. They are called the king of animals because they are so big and strong.

Africa is the place to come to if you want to watch lions.

Lions are the top **predators** in Africa.
They hunt and eat many kinds of animal.
No other animal will hunt a healthy
adult lion.

Africa's Wide-Open Spaces

Africa is the second largest **continent** in the world. Most lions live there. There are some Asian lions in a national park in India. They look very similar to African lions.

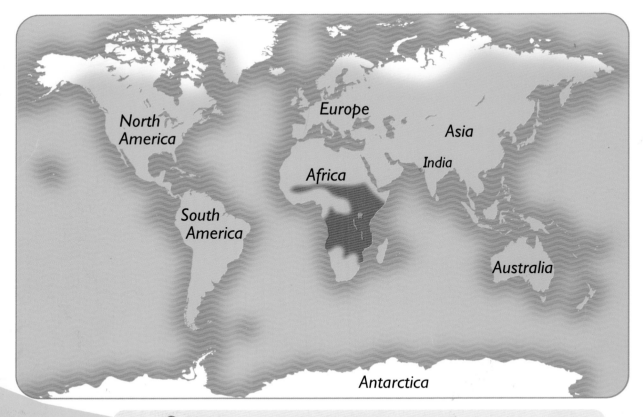

North America

Europe

Asia

India

Africa

South America

Australia

Antarctica

Key ● *This color shows where lions live in Africa and India.*

There are lots of different kinds of land in Africa. Lions live mainly in **savannas**. These are wide-open spaces covered in grass plants. There are some trees and bushes.

Almost half the continent of Africa is covered in savanna like this.

There's a Lion!

It is not always easy to spot lions on the **savanna**. A lion's fur is the same color as the dry, brown grasses.

tail

mane

ears

legs

▲ A male lion has a thick collar of fur around its neck called a mane.

This lion with two cubs is a **female**. Females are smaller than **males** and do not have a mane. Male lions can be as long as a small car.

▲ *All lions are a sandy-brown color.*

Land of the Lions

The savanna has huge areas of grass. Zebra, **wildebeest**, and many other animals come here to **graze**. The lions hunt and eat these animals.

▲ *Grass-eating animals, such as these zebra, live in big groups called **herds**.*

The weather is hot and dry for half the year. During the dry season, it hardly ever rains. Lions often live near a **watering hole**.

▼ *This watering hole has water that the lions can drink almost all year round.*

Seasons in Africa

Africa has two seasons. In the wet season, lots of rain falls. The rain makes lush, green grass grow. Many **herd** animals have their young at this time.

▼ *Lions often chase young animals. Young gazelles cannot run as fast as adults.*

After the big animals leave,
*lions must hunt other **prey**.*

Africa's hot dry season lasts four or five months. At the end of the dry season, the grass is dried up. Many of the big **grazing** animals, such as zebra, leave to find green grass.

13

A Pride of Lions

Lions live together in big groups, or **prides**. Each pride lives and stays in one part of the **savanna**. This is called their **territory**.

▼ *This pride has a mixture of males, females, young lions, and cubs.*

The **male** lions are off on their own. It is their job to protect the **females** and the cubs. They roar loudly to tell other lions to keep off the pride's territory.

You can hear the sound of a lion's mighty roar from far away.

Lazy Lions

At midday, the sun is high in the sky and it is very hot. The lions rest. Most of them sleep in the shade of trees or rocks.

▲ *Lions spend most of the day resting.*

Some of the lions **groom** each other's fur. This makes all the lions in the **pride** smell similar. They can recognize each other by smell, even at night.

▼ *This young lion looks as if it enjoys being groomed.*

Lions Go Hunting

In the evenings, the **female** lions go hunting. They travel until they spot a **herd** of **grazing** animals. The lions sneak up on their **prey**.

▼ *If its prey looks up, the lion will freeze. It is hard to see a lion standing still in the grass.*

As the lions get close to the herd, they pick out one animal to chase. They spread out and surround it. The females work together as a team.

▼ *By working together, these lions can catch animals much bigger than themselves, such as this buffalo.*

Feeding Time

When the **female** lions catch an animal, they grab it with their sharp teeth and big claws. They are lucky if they catch their **prey**. Most lion hunts fail.

Lions must be strong and powerful to bring down a buffalo like this.

The **males** usually follow the hunt. They get to eat first. Then, the females join them. The cubs usually have to wait until last for their turn.

After this big meal, the lions will not need to eat again for two or three days.

Lion Cubs

This **female** lion has had three cubs. Lions are **mammals**. The young cubs feed on milk from their mother's body.

▶▶ *These cubs and their mother are in a safe, hidden spot.*

Feeding time is over, and the mother lion is on the move. She carries the cubs to a new hiding place. Animals such as **hyenas** would eat the cubs if they found them.

▶▶ *It looks uncomfortable, but this mother lion is carrying her cub very gently.*

Growing Up

The older cubs play and fight together. This helps them learn to use their claws and teeth. It gets them ready for when they will have to fight and hunt for real.

▼ *As they play, these cubs are learning to bite, kick, and pounce on* **prey***.*

In the early evening, the cubs follow their mother on a hunting trip. She is showing them how to hunt and to find their way around the **territory**.

When this cub is about a year old, it will start to catch its own prey.

Dangers

Adult lions are the top **predators** in the **savanna**, but they do face some dangers. Zebras can hurt lions by kicking them during a hunt.

⏶ *When young male lions fight they can be badly hurt or even killed.*

People are the biggest danger to lions. They kill lions to protect their farm animals.

Cubs are in danger from leopards and **hyenas**. Even **male** lions from outside the **pride** kill cubs. The cubs that do **survive** could have cubs of their own in a few years.

Tracker's Guide

When you want to watch animals in the wild, you need to find them first. You can look for clues they leave behind.

▶▶ *A lion's paw print looks like a very big cat's!*

◀◀ *Lions scratch marks onto trees or land, just as a house cat scratches a carpet.*

▶▶ *Lions leave dung that trackers can spot.*

Glossary

continent the world is split into seven large areas of land called continents. Each continent is divided into different countries.

female animal that can become a mother when it is grown up. Girls and women are female people.

graze eat grass

groom lick and clean fur

herd group of large, grass-eating animals

hyena dog-like animal that lives on the savanna

male animal that can become a father when it is grown up. Boys and men are male people.

mammal group of animals that feed their babies their own milk and have some hair on their bodies

predator animal that catches and eats other animals for food

prey animal that gets caught and eaten by other animals

pride group of lions

savanna area of land covered mostly in sandy soil and grass, with some trees and bushes

survive stay alive

territory area where an animal lives and feeds

watering hole pool where animals go to drink water

wildebeest kind of large animal with a big head that looks like an ox. A wildebeest is also known as a gnu.

Find Out More

Books

Barnes, Julia. *101 Facts About Lions*. Milwaukee: Gareth Stevens, 2004.

Dineen, Jacqueline. *Lions*. Mankato, Minn.: Smart Apple Media, 2004.

Fox, M. *Continents: Africa*. Chicago: Heinemann Library, 2002.

Kendell, Patricia. *Lions*. Chicago: Raintree, 2002.

Miles, Elizabeth. *Why Do Animals Have Paws and Claws?* Chicago: Heinemann Library, 2002.

Parker, Vic. *We're from Kenya*. Chicago: Heinemann Library, 2005.

Pyers, Greg. *Why Am I a Mammal?* Chicago: Raintree, 2005.

Spilsbury, Louise and Richard. *Life in a Pride: Lions*. Chicago: Heinemann Library, 2004.

Welvaert, Scott R.. *Lions*. Mankato, Minn.: Capstone, 2005.

Index